Discovery

Finding the Hidden Things
I've Always Known

Marni
(Margaret J. Randall)

Discovery | Marni

"A wonderful collection of poems, thoughts and experiences. Marni has been very brave because in this collection she has opened her soul to us ; she has shared her essence with her readers. Some of the works are happy, joyful, others are filled with yearning and beauty, some pieces are sad and almost frightening, yet all are quite exquisite. This collection is well worth reading, and reading slowly and meditating on. Thank you Marni, your readers will be left deeply moved at your thoughts, thanks for sharing your life experiences with us."
—Alison Lewis, author of *Missing* & *Seasons of Life*

"Marni unabashedly takes the reader on a trip through her lifecycle, sharing her story so openly. The poems are raw with pain, longing and questioning, but also with hope and wonderment — of love, family, religion, self."
— Natalie Vujovich, author of *Where Did I Leave My Dragon?*

"People everywhere around the world use different methods of escaping from the reality of their lives. Some look for love while others just want to imagine a new reality for themselves.

This book of poetry is based on a whole life of musings, escapism and trying to find the answer to many questions I am sure we have all asked ourselves. Not just a 'book of poetry' this collection from Marni, the author, is rather beautiful and haunting in some places while others are stark and lonely.

Marni has written her poetry to coincide with short life stories which she shares with us. Forgotten moments in time when she remembers sharing a bathroom with her parents and looking balefully at their false teeth in a glass; being mesmerised by the show of affection between her best friend and her mother (a thing unknown to her); trapped in a loveless marriage; and even poems to her soulmate.

Full of whimsy, charm and recollections, Marni's life is laid bare for us all to become acquainted with her. Her poetry and writings have soul and this charming book also includes sketches which adorn the book throughout.

I love her introduction where she describes her poems as 'stops along the way to take in the view' which is a wonderful way to describe a life. This collection is a rare find nowadays; sensitive, quirky and thought-provoking.

This warm, sometimes sad but always entertaining book of poetry follows the author's journey through a life filled with 'many stops along the way'."

—John Morrow's *Pick of the Week*

This collection of poetry, commentary and thoughts is drawn from a lifetime of observation and discovery of the unspoken knowledge that's always been with me. In this book you'll find humour, joy and pain. I do hope you'll find it an engaging read.

Published in Australia by Sid Harta Publishers Pty Ltd,
ABN: 46 119 415 842

23 Stirling Crescent, Glen Waverley, Victoria 3150 Australia

Telephone: +61 3 9560 9920, Facsimile: +61 3 9545 1742

E-mail: author@sidharta.com.au

First published in Australia 2018

This edition published 2018

Copyright © Marni (Margaret J. Randall) 2018

Cover design, typesetting: WorkingType (www.workingtype.com.au)

The right of Marni (Margaret J. Randall) to be identified as the Author of the Work has been asserted in accordance with the Copyright, Designs and Patents Act 1988.

All rights reserved. No part of this publication may be reproduced, stored in a retrieval system, or transmitted, in any form or by any means without the prior written permission of the publisher, nor be otherwise circulated in any form of binding or cover other than that in which it is published and without a similar condition being imposed on the subsequent purchaser.

Marni (Margaret J. Randall)
Discovery — Finding the Hidden Things I've Always Known
ISBN: 978-1-925230-38-3
pp176

With grateful thanks

to

my grandson Sebastian, the computer expert,

my daughter Christine, the Word expert,

and my son Clinton, the organisational expert,

whose combined efforts helped pull my computer into some kind of coherence.

I began writing poems in childhood, simply to record my

feelings and experiences,

    so these poems are

        like stops on the way

            to take in the view ~

Contents

Untasted Love 4
My Mother's Corsets 6
The Toothy Grin with No Face Around It 8
Spirit of Wonder 10
You 14
Silence 15
Memories 16
Response 19
Love Incarnate 20
A Letter to My Soul-Mate 21
Deep Water 25
Enlightenment 30
Glorious Enigma 35
Enlightenment — a Postscript 36
Everywhere I Go 38
Holy Hologram 40
By the Sauna 44
Dappled Shadow 46
Dead Heart 47
Only Then 51
Strange Ambivalence! 52
The Perfumed Garden 54
Old Lovers 55
Julie at the Opera House 56
Summer Rain 59
Meditation 61
The Me Tree 63
Siamese Twins 65
Trivia 66
An Arcane Adventure 67
Morning Meditation 76

Play of Fear	79
Two-Way Mirror	83
See Ya!	84
The Key to the Theory of Everything	86
Now	88
Beyond the Biological Computer	89
City Streets	91
Munda Nyuringu	93
Fellow Traveller	96
Passacaglia	99
Moonlight	101
Camping with Rambo	103
On the Dual Sexuality of the Common Garden Snail	106
The Gardener	108
Walking the Desert	110
Moonshine Magic	112
Metaphors and Mysteries	114
Delphic Oracle	120
Light	122
Linked Haiku	124
Dreams	125
Daemons	128
They Say	132
The Clay Statuette	133
In Winter in Mallacoota	139
Guru	144
Cronesong	145
When I Was Young	146
Peripeteia	149
Confumony	150
In the Arms of Thanatos	152
Being Myself	154
Recognition	155
Lesser Gods	157
Luminescence	158
?	163

Foreword

While the fabric of my life has a few fancy designs woven through the cloth, the strong lengthwise threads express my ever-present desire to understand, to wonder, to find some meaning in this thing we call life — my search for ultimate truth. So you will find here many questions together with a few answers, which aren't really answers of course, but pointers towards the truth.

Woven through these threads is my desire for true intimacy, so long denied me. Here are the passionate dreams of a quiet, shy girl; and here, too, the mature yearnings of a woman, locked for twenty-one years in a loveless and violent marriage — and eventually, freed from all this, my exploration of a genuine relationship, and the coming of peace.

You will find here the pain of being alone in an indifferent world, the joy of union and the pain of separation. Add a tiny touch of humour, a few threads of observation, and you have my book. This is the warp and woof of a very small piece of cloth; but it is the fabric of my being.

Sometimes I hear
    the faintest echo
    of forgotten melody,
    and as I move to follow
    it disappears,
        a vanished whisper of memory
            – a wisp of longing.

I know
    there are treasures
    I have forgotten,
        and one day
            I will remember . . .

I was born knowing something. The trouble was I didn't know that I knew it. It sat like a kind of inner authority, surfacing at times to thrill at the approach of the numinous, at other times to announce that this is WRONG!

My mother told me that when I was born her gynaecologist, Dr Agnes Donaldson, held me up as she announced, "She's been here before!" Just her fanciful idea perhaps, but the knowledge carried me through my childhood and adolescence, and helped me emerge beyond my father's angry beatings (pants down, bare bottom across his knees) with my self-esteem more or less intact.

I never really understood what made him so angry, but hindsight brought some understanding. My mother had recoiled from my father in disgust at the whole process of procreation, and they shared the house in a state of almost-silent almost-truce.

He was about to beat me again when I was around sixteen or seventeen, when Mum appeared at the door and asked — napalm eyes and ice-dagger voice — "I think she's a bit old for that now, don't you?" It was a threat, not a question, and he never tried it again. There was no love in the house, and my poem here describes my experience of growing up:

Untasted Love

I never knew my mother's kisses –
    did she kiss me when I was small?
I walk with my memories
    all the way back to babyhood –
    but I find no kisses there,
no caresses.

How many millions down the centuries
    have cried for this
    in unexplored regions of the heart —
        this untasted love,
            longed for,
        embracing you as a cherished member
        of the family.

I became a stoic.

Now I wonder:
    Did some small, unheard part of me
        feel emotionally naked?
    Unprotected?
    Cheated of my birth-right?

A teenager,
    I felt like an orphan,
        and yet . . .
My mother worked hard,
    provided healthy food,
    good clothes.
I used to wonder
    was this her way of expressing love,
        or merely her strong sense of duty?
    I often wondered . . .

When she died,
    we found a note in her writing desk:
"I was never demonstrative,"
    she said,
    "but I did love you."

Mum took me on a visit to our country relations, and I remember sharing a bedroom, and a bed, during our stay:

My Mother's Corsets

In the dark I hear
    the *whirr-r-whirr-ir-r* of laces
    being drawn through eyelets
    in my mother's
    salmon pink corsets.

Long laces,
    easing, loosening;
    then a soft thud
    as the whole monstrosity
    is dropped on the floor.

Holidays . . .

A drowsy three year old
    has been slipped into this big, soft bed,
    to lie awake
    staring at shadows
    whispering across the ceiling,
    sliding silently
    over alien furniture.

Stealthy rustlings as my mother enters,
    starts to undress,
    and the laces begin to whirr.
Her body, released at last
    into its natural plumpness,
    flops into the bed
    with great tuggings and pullings
    of sheets and blankets.
Arrows of icy air stab into my cosy nest,
    until the now-safe dark
    envelops our two bodies
    in a feather-down quilt of comfort . . .

Snap!   Slap!!
My eyes open in the gold-and-silver
    half-light of early morning,
    to the slapping and snapping of whale-bone.
My mother's body is being constrained once more
        into its daily prison.

Early memories of my mother are loud
    with *whirr* and *snap* and *slap*,
    and visions of long, strong
    salmon pink corsets.

Our shared family bathroom brought an intimacy I found distasteful at times, although I tried not to show it.

The Toothy Grin with No Face Around It

I still remember that toothy grin –
    no face around it,
    just water in a glass.
They gave me the creeps,
    those gummy teeth
    – like body parts,
        smugly smiling.

I didn't want to kiss my parents
    because that was where
    those gooey teeth lived.
Somehow I just *knew* they were slimy.
And I knew little bits of yucky food
    still clung to them, too.
Revulsion made my stomach heave.

So when the dentist threatened me recently,
> saying, "You may need to have
> some of those teeth out" –
>> suddenly I knew
>> how it must have been
>> for my parents.
I was glad then I never told them
> how I felt
> about those toothy, watery grins
> with no face around them.

My best friend in those early days was Gwenda Jacobs. When I was around five years old, I was invited to stay with her family in their log cabin in Lockwood. I was mystified one evening when her mother was sitting in an armchair by the log fire, and Gwenda climbed into her lap for a hug and cuddles.

I had felt the same awkwardness a year or two earlier at kindergarten, when the teacher tried to sit me on her lap. I struggled down and ran outside to play with the others. I was really fond of her and it made me sad, feeling that 'now she'll think I don't like her'. I didn't know how to respond to love — I hadn't had any practice.

Gwenda appears in the next poem:

Spirit of Wonder

Little Girl, blue eyes wide,
    is staring, fascinated, at a dewdrop.
If she turns her head this way,
    she finds a rainbow in the droplet;
    and if she shifts her weight
    the tiniest fraction
    to the other leg,
    it sparkles with white light
    like a diamond.
Then she discovers
    the whole lawn is sprinkled with diamonds.

She knows, this little girl,
    that on the bluestone in the back lane
    grows moss like deep green velvet.
Sometimes she runs her finger over it
    very gently,
    loving the feel of its bouncy softness.
Sometimes, too, she lies on her back
    staring at the blue sky:
    you know what?
If you use your eyes just right,
    you can see what the air's made of!

Last week, Little Girl
    played at her girlfriend's place,
    and the air rippled with their laughter.
They climbed the pussy willow tree,
    and stroked the tiny catkins:
    'They feel like little kittens –
    let's call them kitkins!'

Climbing trees is the best fun.
She has discovered,
    in her blue-eyed wonder,
    that the almond tree
    has the prettiest blossom in the world.

Once, holidaying with her friend
    in the country,
    they found a fairy-ring!
There, in the crackling dry bushland,
    was a perfect circle
    of the softest, greenest grass
    – all smooth as if it had just been mown –
    and surrounding it,
    a ring of the daintiest toadstools.
It couldn't have happened just by chance,
    could it?
'There must be fairies!'

Little Girl has become a grandmother:
> now there is Little Boy,
> all of seven years old –
> a busy little fellow.

After school there's basketball training,
> and cello lessons,
> and swimming lessons,
> and cello practice,
> and at weekends, basketball matches –
> "I hope we win this week!"

Best of all, when there's time,
> there's the computer,
>> and
> (*dah-dah!*) — Nintendo!

He's so quick –
> much faster than Mum or Dad,
> and they're really quick.

He can win all the games,
> and solve all the puzzles.

But he's never noticed the jewels in a dew-drop,
    or felt the velvety moss in the back lane,
    or stared at the sky
    seeing what the air's made of.
And he's never stood in a fairy ring,
    or stroked the kitkins
    on the pussy willow tree.
He's like all seven year old boys:
    too busy for the spirit of wonder.

My disastrous marriage brought three children,
but only two poems:

You

    You carry your own world with you –
        nothing external impinges on it.
    Perhaps this is not bad, if your world is large and fine,
        something transcending normal prosaic affairs.
    But your world is small, the size of your one self only.
    Indeed, you are so self-oriented in your restless way,
        I have to shout to make myself heard
        above the clamour of your jangling ego.

    The best of me is quiet, responsive, and unable to shout.
    So the deep quiet wells within me
        have never been encountered by you;
        and I resent the screaming monster
        you try to force me to become.
    Be that, or be ignored.

    I think I prefer to be ignored,
        but by you only . . .
    Those wells of quietness remain, for one who has eyes to see.

    Waiting for discovery.

Silence

Your silence is too noisy.
It fills the air with anger, irritation,
    frets my ears with its screeching discords.

And so, denied calm solitude,
    I tune the radio to gentle harmony,
    and search for peace . . .

There is a little bit of the Cinderella in all of us perhaps, hoping that one day our prince (or princess) will come, and my knowingness told me that the relationship I longed for was possible, maybe imminent. So my yearning found words, all mixed up, of course, with the normal desires of a young girl. Locked in a loveless marriage, I waited and dreamed, and putting my feelings on paper seemed to bring release, making them real and tangible. I poured all the longings, hopes and dreams of my young life into these poems:

Memories

Can anyone understand the pain in my heart now?
It is quivering like newly-cut flesh.
Bleeding.
You ask me why?
Surely, you think
    it cannot be just because I am alone!

For you believe I am alone
    only in this one small moment of time.
You cannot comprehend
    the utter isolation of my soul.

I have family, friends.
Every day my life touches the lives of others –
    or rather almost touches;
    but not quite,
    for they are all alone too.
All wrapped up in their own little solitudes,
    and they do not remember . . .

Once there was love.
Oh — it was not in this life,
    but faint memories are there
    to disquiet the surface of my mind .
I feel, if I try very hard,
    the memory must come back clearly
    in all its tender detail.

Such sharing of souls it was — no mere physical ecstasy!
No rapture of a moment,
    followed by a great weariness of heart;
    but every moment giving,
    giving,
    and receiving equally.
And every moment of giving creating new rapture.

Such gentleness was there!
Such one-ness!
We were one soul,
    yet each retaining our identity
    in order to give again . . .

Why were we torn apart?
What vast logic has decreed that we must walk alone?
And why now, this dreary life half-spent,
    is my soul still hungry for that other love?

Oh, all you other souls
    whose lives meet and part in this little life,
    did you never know such love?
And are you never hungry
    to taste it once again?
You seem so immersed in the busy-ness of living,
    you've forgotten what Life is!

Do the ripples of memory
    never disturb the quiet waters of your complacency?
        . . . or are there moments in your solitude, too,
    when your soul cries out
    for that which you do not understand?

Am I one with all humanity in this search
    for a love I can almost remember –
    and should I, in my agony,
    pity you in yours?
        – or –

    am I truly alone?

Response

    'Not eros of the body, but eros of the soul' — Plato.

Is there a greater joy than to give oneself
    knowing the gift's desired?
Sex becomes a physical symbol
    of the thrill of sharing souls.
A spiritual ecstasy.

Your mind throbs and flows
    into the mind of the loved one,
    and, in return, receives the loved one's mind with joy.
The tender play of mind on mind,
        heart on heart,
        emotion on emotion,
    carries an intermingling of the spirit –
    a unity whose orgasm never dies.
Two souls become one, yet never cease to be separate.
What rapture would there be
    if they became completely one –
    can one drop in a pool of water
    give pleasure to another?
Only in constant giving and receiving
    does pleasure lie.
So . . .

You are you,
        and I am I –
Shall we explore this joy together?

Love Incarnate

Come, take my hand, and let me feel the soft caress
    of your lips dreaming against mine, and press
    your throbbing body against my yearning softnesses.

Dear one, our love becomes incarnate,
    and, like all mortal things,
    thrills with life, and flames with rapture
    for a little space.
And, like all fleshly things
    must pass without a trace –
    pass, to be born anew, and live in thrilling pain
    – and die again.

And does our tender love thus wax and wane?
Ah no! For love itself is one of the immortals –
    the one true lovely thing
    which draws us to the portals
    of life eternal.

When we love truly, we are most like gods,
    and nearest our intended destiny.

So, take my hand, and show me, in physical expression
    that deep eternal love we both have in possession.

A Letter to My Soul-Mate

I feel I know that once there was one soul -
    just one creation, perfect and complete.
Until some great primeval force
    split my soul in two,
    and sent it's separate parts
    wandering through the timeless years,
    and through the endless space of infinite universes
    each doomed to search alone,
    and yearns and ache
    until they find each other once again.

I feel I know that you and I are one.
And if you turn from me, you will go on
    to search again
    and ache and yearn still more until,
    like two small atoms blown together once again
        (by chance perhaps, or some strange power?)
    we meet once more
        (some other world maybe, some other life?)
    and you, at last,
    in some bright flash of recognition,
    know your own soul when thus we meet,
    and we rejoice!

Discovery | Marni

> I am but half a woman
> — you half a man —
> until, in union, we shall find our own true selves,
> our joys, our powers,
> and our nobility.

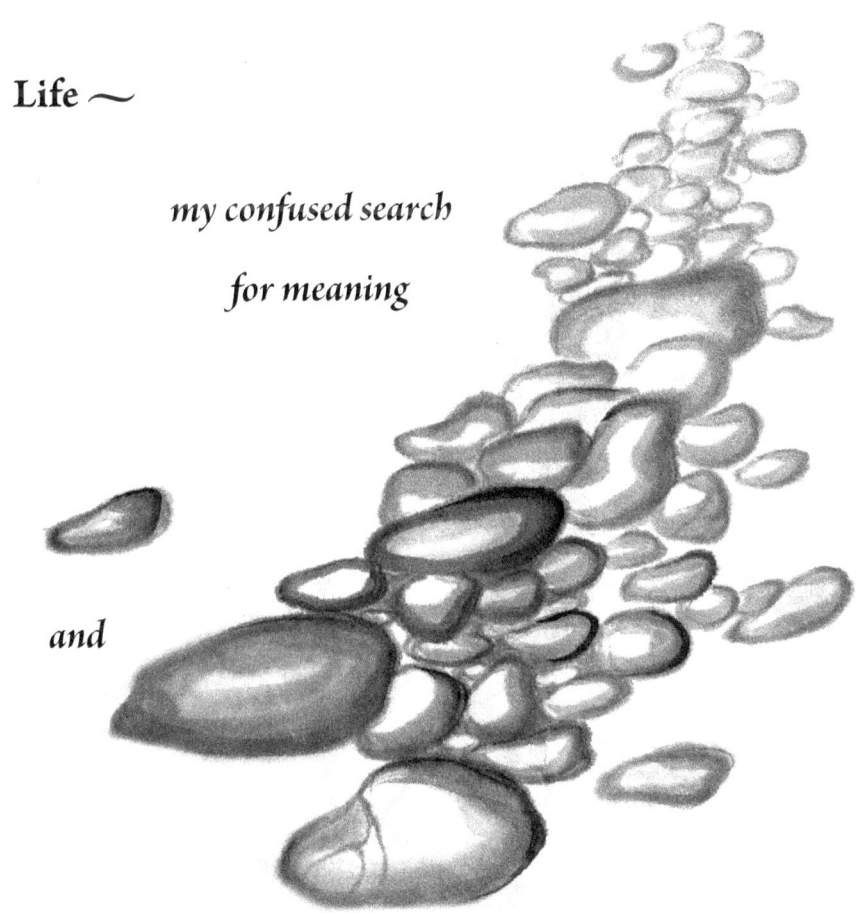

Life ~

    my confused search

       for meaning

and

    the path to understanding

I was born knowing something. The trouble was I didn't know that I knew it. But beyond all my dreaming, the knowingness flowed like a steady undercurrent beneath the surface of my mind. It ran under all my daily activities and experiences, as if I was floating on top of something very important, something holding me up:

Deep Water

The water is deep and warm.
When I swim, I feel it moving — soft — against my skin.
    and when I float — relaxed — I am gentled
    on its smoothly lapping surface.

The ripples on this surface glimmer and glint.
They are bright, moving lights
    dancing with black shadows;
    but they live, and dance, only on the surface:
    bright mirrors reflecting the world around,
    and giving no hint
    of the quiet depths beneath.

If you reach deep, deep down
    beyond those sparkling ripples,
    if you really dive deep enough, you may
        – perhaps –
    find the well-springs of eternal joy.

Why not?

Go now!

    Down,

        down

into the depths of your very being,

through the swirling, unknown currents

of that shadowy, watery world,

where only small, misty patches of light

guide you past its strange denizens.

Searching . . .

    searching for those springs

    which are always flowing,

        constant,

            serene.

    And if you find them

        you will know yourself.

Deep Water

As I grew older, I was gradually becoming aware of a search for that something missing — the search for the beloved. I looked for the answer in religion — after all, I had a church background — and I became very devout for a time. But then that inner authority would assert itself. There are memories of sitting in choir as a teenager and hearing the preacher's voice, while above that came the still small voice within telling me that this, or that, is WRONG!

So my religion became eclectic: accepting what I felt was right, and discarding what I knew to be wrong. It wasn't working. I looked at other denominations, other religions — but always I came up against rules. To be an adherent, this is what you must believe, this is what we don't accept. They left no room for my inner authority; it was like a spiritual straitjacket.

I gradually lost contact with the church, but became quite concerned during the 1960s, when the media began disseminating a lot of anti-Muslim material, long before the current violence. And yes, they told horrific stories, but I compared these with stories I'd heard about the Inquisition, and equally terrible behaviour sanctioned by the Christian church.

I remembered my early life: taken to church and Sunday school, hearing the Bible stories; and I thought a Muslim would have grown up being taken to a mosque and reading the Koran. Religion, it seemed, was going to extremes and using it as an excuse for violence — a violence which probably stems from our innate fear of being alone in the universe. I was feeling like a rudderless ship venturing into a stormy sea, with nothing to guide me other than my inner knowing. But that knowing told me that beyond all this there is an ultimate Truth — and that Truth was what I was searching for.

I read a huge number of books — some of them helped, but none revealed the essential core of my search. I was like a young girl yearning for her lover, only my lover wasn't a human being, and while I want to say I was longing for God, that name carries too much baggage. I once heard Deepak Chopra describe God as a non-material loving Intelligence, and that was as close as I could get to it, but it wasn't enough.

I learned to live with a deep yearning in my heart. It remained like an ostinato beyond my daily activities — beyond running the household, beyond mothering my three children; even beyond the sheer terror I lived with during my twenty-one year marriage to a narcissistic psychotic, and my escape from it.

Strangely, before that escape came the most profound experience of my life.

It was a sunny spring morning, and Nature's rejoicing must have somehow infused my soul with peace. My son was at kindergarten, the two girls at school, and I'd gone upstairs to make my daughter's bed:

Enlightenment

Perhaps only those who have experienced this will understand: I had glimpsed, briefly, how it feels to exist as pure consciousness. When I returned to the space/time continuum, it took some time to adjust!

It is warm here in the attic bedroom.
Through the open window I hear birds
    discovering their spring songs,
      and the window is bright with late morning sunshine.
I spread the sheets on my daughter's bed,
    and smooth them flat.
I draw up the blankets and pull out the creases,
    and I am suddenly
        utterly lost in You.

Lost in a dream,
    except this dream is more real
    than anything I once called reality.
That one-time, old-time reality
    has ceased to exist.
My soul is all gossamer,
    ebbing and flowing serenely
    with the pulse of Your Being.
I am immersed in You –
    Your Being is an ocean,
    and I am drifting,
        dissolving in love.

I feel Your Being streaming
> gently through me
> and I am suffused with Love and Joy,
> – glowing within.

I know only You and me,
> flowing together.

There is only Now . . .

Now?
Now I'm sitting on a bed –
> which bed?

What is this body –
> it sits heavy on my gossamer soul!

Which body?
> Who?
>> Where?
>>> When?

I'm totally lost in this strange reality.

I know only the dream
> only You.

I don't recognise this strange flesh,
> this place,
>> this — time?

I am besieged by questions,
> lost in an alien world,
> struggling to find my way.

Now slowly . . . very slowly
   the mist rises, and the answers come.
Slowly, gropingly, I remember:
   I have a name,
      a year,
         a family,
           a home in this other reality.
   I am no longer lost.

The mist drifts,
   settles behind me
      over the place whence I have come.
But now — I KNOW!
That which I had only suspected
   – or hoped –
   I know

I know I am supremely, identifiably myself
   – always.
Unique.
Complete.
I AM ME! FOREVER!!
But that me is inseparably part of You.
I know all life, all creation, is part of You:
   You are composed of all created life
      in the same way as my body
         is composed of its own separate, conscious cells.

Yet the whole is greater
    than the sum of its parts –
You are more than the sum total of all creation.
    and I am one with all creation,
        because each one of us is a tiny part of You!
Oh, that knowledge fills me with joy!
I am radiant!!!

The rubbish men are clattering bins and lids
    outside in the spring sun.
How you'd laugh, I think,
    if I told you you're part of God –
    but it's true!
Their voices sound a harsh counterpoint
    to the birds' happy descant.

The school bell rings.
But it can't be!
I've been gone forever –
    aeons,
        centuries,
            . . . was it really only minutes?
How many minutes?
    I don't know.

This afternoon as I walk down the street,
    strangers turn and smile
    as if we're old friends,
      and I am overflowing with joy.
Of course we're all friends,
      only some of us know it,
           . . . and some have forgotten.

This must have happened more than fifty years ago. I remember it was springtime, and Clinton (my son) was in kindergarten — he's now in his mid-fifties.

Glorious Enigma

'Enlightenment'– the Now of the Experience

Like a wisp of seaweed
    drifting in the flowing currents,
    so am I flowing in this ocean of love.

I have no borders,
    no edges,
    time and space suspended
    I am one with the ocean.
Intrinsically part of the ocean,
       yet –

Somewhere within this familiar mystery
    I also feel myself filled with glowing intensity,
    and with the wondrous awareness that
    I am experiencing
    this glorious enigma.

Enlightenment — a Postscript

Right now, I feel rather like a little child at Christmas time,
    or maybe waiting for a party.
Only there's nothing on the calendar
    to explain my sense of eager expectancy.

I wish I knew what this special feeling is,
    why it's descended on me out of the blue.
Does my subconscious know something
    my conscious mind isn't aware of?

I feel as if something wonderful lies in store for me,
    but I'm groping blindly,
        trying to understand just what it is.
Ah — THAT'S IT!
That's how I feel now:
    like a blind man who knows,
        without seeing,
    that there's something out there.
And in the same way I know,
        without understanding,
    that something wonderful exists for me.

Enlightenment — a Postscript

I feel myself moving towards this special thing,
    hurrying, eager to find whatever it is –
    to know what it is;
    but I'm not frantically excited like the birthday child.

Can you imagine this joyful anticipation
    experienced with serenity?
That's how I feel now.

And every day is my birthday.

Everywhere I Go

Everywhere I go
> I search for You.

I seek You
> in everyone I meet.

You are glowing in the flowers.
> and flowing in the river.

I feel You blowing in the breeze.

Everywhere I go
> I search for You.

I see You
> in everyone I meet.

I want to understand my Enlightenment experience. If we really are like cells in the body of God, then as long as God exists, we exist — surrounded and filled by the same infinity of loving energy as I experienced then. There was no teaching, no instruction; I just *knew* what I was experiencing.

I wrote then:
> 'You are composed of all created life
> in the same way as my body
> is composed of its own separate, conscious cells . . .

... and I am one with all creation,
because each one of us is a tiny part of You!'

I feel it's telling me that my energy, and the energy of all life, is part of God. It's not that God created us, but that we are part of the one overarching energy. There are profound implications here. It suggests that always, in all situations, I am spirit — and that within all memories, all lifetimes, I remain this conscious energy.

Does this mean that we all hold elements of the divine within us? That we simply need to recognise our own inner splendour? Do we need to experience our utter aloneness in this world, before we're capable of reaching deep enough to find our own personal glory? Maybe separation and suffering are a necessary part of the journey!

And what about other forms of life — are dogs and prehistoric monsters and microbes also part of God? Are they busy evolving too? My friend John believes that we live through many lifetimes, 'bound on the wheel' as the Buddhists say. But to what end? I feel there must be some point, some meaning to all this suffering — until we reach a state of cosmic consciousness, John says. Perhaps we all begin in the same way, and it's up to us to evolve to that point.

Maybe we're all little gods in the making! (Even microbes and monsters!)

Perhaps suffering brings us the understanding we need in order to evolve. And because we're all open to suffering of some kind or other, my inner knowing, along with my Enlightenment experience, reassures me that I am at least on the path, however slow and painful the journey.

Holy Hologram

What an enigma!

Within a shattered hologram
    each fragment will repeat,
    unbroken and undamaged –
    the image perfect and complete.

So remember when you feel
    your heart is broken
    – or your soul –
    that you are part of God
    and know that you are whole.

You are whole
    dreaming the life you're living now.

But what if this life you're living now,
    and all the lives you've ever lived,
    are simply dreams:
        pleasant dreams,
            confused dreams
    – nightmares?!

Remember . . .
    Dreams fade quickly
        once you wake.
Remember . . .
    You are the Dreamer,
        not the dream.

    You are the Dreamer
    dreaming the life you're living now.

    Remember Who you are

Discovery | Marni

Old Buddhist Adage

Before Enlightenment —
                carry water, pick up sticks:
After Enlightenment —
                carry water, pick up sticks.

By the Sauna

The feel of grass, warm and damp beneath my legs,
    happy glow of sun on my skin.
Little giggles of water come to my ears,
    rippling through reeds by the river bank,
    disconnected snatches of bird song.

My body feels and hears these things,
    and knows peace.
It sends messages to headquarters about its position,
    for I am not there.
I am everywhere.

Gems gleam and disappear
    as sun discovers dew-damp grass,
    sparkles on gum tips,
    shiny and new-born.
Smell of sun-hot grass
    musky scent of fresh smoke.

My body sees and smells,
    duly reporting to headquarters,
    for I am not there.
I am everywhere.

By the Sauna

Behind my back,
    sun shines on a sauna
    lovingly built with rounded river rocks
    growing peacefully from the landscape.
Cows graze luxuriously
    in the paddock across the way.

My body is telling me about it's one small spot in space,
    but I'm not only there with my body –
    I am everywhere,
        there,
            and here too.

Dappled Shadow

Sitting in dappled shadow,
    legs in sun,
    I'm immersed in a peaceful polyphony of nature:
    threads of tiny twitterings
    interweaving through cooing of doves,
    screech of a raven.

Motionless,
    the paraphernalia of nature
    flows into my body
    as if by osmosis.
One with the natural world.

"Sometimes,"
    a friend once told me,
"I feel my heart
 glowing like a great ball,
 swelling fit to burst
 with pure, unfocussed Love."

Yes, I remember.
That same ball is glowing now within me,
    reaching out,
    welcoming the world.
Now I know.

Dead Heart

Parched earth,
    gritty on your fingertips.
No life there it seems –
        arid.
The spinifex looks dead too,
    it's so dry.
Stunted scrub, barely subsisting.

Hot rocks reflect the sun,
    and you can smell the heat.
It moves with you, this airless heat,
    sapping your energy.
Overpowering.

Look — there's a dead branch . . .
Seems to me it's always been dead,
    like it would burst into flame
    as soon as you look at it,
        as if all it needs is the power of your sight
        to burn to ashes.
Skin's burning dry too –
    feels like you might burst into flame.

It's a bit like the atmosphere
    people create between each other:
  relationships arid,
        dry –
            dead.
Sometimes you think there's never been life there,
    they're so accustomed to aridity.
Perhaps they're afraid of clouds;
        but
    have you ever seen the desert after rain?

A brush, loaded with green paint,
    has swept across the landscape;
    and suddenly it's bursting with life.
The brush has spread drifts of colour everywhere too:
    brilliant flowers flaunt their beauty,
    while shy delicate ones,
    hide in secret hollows.

From nowhere, it seems,
    clouds of birds arrive in their thousands,
    crying, cackling around the lakes.
Those same lakes which,
      for years,
    have opened their private parts
    – dry and cracked to the scorching sky –
    now spread their shimmering mirrors
    to capture this amazing sudden beauty.

There are spangles of puddles
    filled with life:
        fish,
            frogs,
                insects too.
Where did they come from?
Was there life hidden in that gritty soil,
    waiting for the blessing of water?

So tears of the soul are shed
    when one soft caress,
    one tender word,
    one gentle kiss bestowed with love,
    falls like gentle rain.
And a look, soaking beneath that crusty surface,
    finds the soul.
Then the miracle of love floods the brush with colour
    to spread smiles
        happiness
        – peace.

Where do they come from?
Were they always there, lying
    dormant,
        unrecognised,
            shrivelled under the desert sun?
Waiting for the blessing of love!

Only Then . . .

Only when we draw so close in our hearts,
> that our souls whisper to each other,
> only then do we understand love.

There are men who,
> knowing so little of truth,
> claim they can *make* love.

They are lost to its infinite pleasures.

For we who love know
> it is only when we draw so close in our hearts
> that our souls whisper to each other,
>> only then
>
> can we say we truly love.

Strange Ambivalence!

Did we meet and love
    in some previous life?

Do we, even now,
    meet and love
    – somewhere –
    in a parallel universe?

My soul knows something
    my mind cannot comprehend . . .

Many times, sitting behind you in philosophy class,
    my hand has ached to touch your soft, soft hair
    (is it really as soft as it looks?)

Your eyes tell me things your mouth has never said.
Your words remain distant,
    yet your touch welcomes me –
    makes me feel I have come home
    where I belong.

Strange ambivalence!
Our separate worlds are moving in different directions,
    and briefly their orbits meet.
I hear your words
    and add my own
    across a gulf of our own making, yet –
you are home.

Strange ambivalence!
Knowing we love,
    yet knowing it cannot be.
I sense your trajectory moving away from me,
    and do not ask to change it –
    only to love while we are close.
Or would such meeting cause a collision
    that would shake the universe?

Strange ambivalence indeed!
Your nearness is peace.

The Perfumed Garden

We never made any children together,
    you and I.
But sometimes, when I cut your hair,
    I swept up the clippings
    and put them in the compost bin
    along with my own.

And it all rotted and blended together
    – your peelings and mine –
    along with the vegetable peelings
    (and the herb tea bags, and the dead flowers).

I used to spread the beautiful, rich black soil it became
    around the plants in the garden;
    and of course, I used lots of it
    when I planted new ones.

So now, when I walk in my garden
    brilliant with cheeky blooms,
    or discover shy delicate ones
    hiding in a corner
        – when I smell their fragrance
        drifting in the sunlight –
    then I know I am walking amongst our children,
    yours and mine,
    and breathing their beauty.

Old Lovers

There should be stars in the eyes of old lovers:
    starlight catches your heart,
    unfolds your mind.

But the stars spun their light aeons ago –
    where are they now?
Old stars are just dead rocks!

Old lovers should look at each other
    with stars in their eyes,
    filling them with remembrance
    seeing beyond the ravages of time,
    to seek the light shining still
    within each other's hearts.

Perchance to find the light
    of a yesterday they never knew.

Starlight catches your heart
    and unfolds your mind –
        there should be stars in the eyes
        of old lovers.

Julie at the Opera House

1973 — after a visit to the Sydney Opera House to hear my friend, Julie Raines, play.

Sound pearls, gentle as rippling water,
    are floating from the great golden harp.
The hall is full of people,
    and there is a breath of expectancy.
They are waiting for the pearls.

Now they are everywhere, those pearls,
    floating through the air,
    spinning,
    twisting and turning;
    some transparent as bubbles,
    their surfaces glistening with iridescent colours.
Dropping now, slowly,
    softly as snowflakes.

At the harp, a slender girl,
    long hair shining in the spotlight,
    golden as the harp.
She plucks the strings softly
    and a cascade, liquid as water,
    ripples through the hall.
And now, more crisply:
    instantly the pearls are gone.

Instead — gemstones.
Sparkling, brilliant colours
    shoot from the harp,
    and fly into the air.
They speed around the concert hall,
    then fall to the ears of the listening crowd.

The people are spell-bound.
Crystal stars are falling all over the hall,
    like rain.

Long, slender fingers move
    swiftly over the strings.
Graceful.
A fold of soft, blue fabric
    shines in the spotlight,
    as full, blue sleeves float rhythmically,
    like gentle waves on a summer sea.
She is all grace,
    so completely lost in her music
    that her soul flies,
    sparkling with the gems
    as they twist and turn.
Her gift to them all –
    her soul.

Now the gems are gone too,
    and only bubbles remain.
They float,
    shine,
        hover, and pause:
            then, one by one, wink out.
There is nothing left.

Only the golden-haired girl alone on the stage,
    empty –
    the hall silent,
        expectant,
            hushed . . .

Then — the storm!
Like a furious wave
    it crashes over the hall.
The people, woken from their dream,
    are tumultuous.
The thunder,
    huge,
    overbearing,
    reaches the golden-haired girl . . .
She stirs, smiles,
    and gathers in her soul.

Then she stands,
    and the spotlight follows her
    as she moves forward centre stage,
    and bows.

Summer Rain

This morning I will take my breakfast
    out to the back porch,
    and watch the misty rain fall
    like a bridal veil over my dry garden,
    and the park beyond.

I will see leaves tremble
    at its touch,
    flowers lift their faces
    to be washed;
    and slow drops fall like pearls
    from the fronds of weeping wattle.

I will see small ripples come and go
    on the surface of the bird bath;
    and brief bubbles, like tiny rainbows,
    appear and vanish there.

I will breathe the perfume of grateful earth,
    and hear the song of plants,
    as their searching roots find
    the essence of life in the now-dark soil,
    while clear air carries
    the ripple of bird song.

Discovery | Marni

I will hear the song of plants,
    and the song of birds
        blending with the song of the earth.

I will hear
    and smell
        and see the Symphony of Nature.
And my soul will sing!

Meditation

Listen to the Now . . .

Listen,
    hear the sounds of Now
        seeking my attention?
The train rumbling into a station,
    snatches of bird song,
        muted roar of traffic
            charging along a distant highway?

Listen to the Now of a bee
    as it hums lazily by,
    a tiny leaf
    rustling in the whisper of a breeze.

Forget the sounds of yesterday –
    they are gone.
And who can tell what will be
    the sounds of tomorrow?

Discovery | Marni

    I hear only the sounds of this moment
        as I sit motionless,
            relaxed,
                erect,
                    winter sun warm on my skin –
                        part of the Now of Creation
                        flowing around me . . .

    I merge with the Now,
        and become one with all that is.

The Me Tree

I had planted this lemon-scented eucalypt in the park outside my home.

This tree is me . . .
Because there is no time
> this tree is me,
> experiencing my Godself
> when I was less aware of that Self within.

Once, when my tree self was a mere sapling,
> a lout of a boy on a bike
>> (who is and was also my Godself
>> in a less aware human form)
> grabbed my tree self,
> twisted it,
> and broke it off at ground level.

From my kitchen window,
> I looked at the empty place in the park
> where my tree self had been,
> and mourned its passing.

But I knew my tree self was not dead,
    so I sent it encouragement:
    every day I looked at the tiny stump,
    and told it what a beautiful tree it was,
        and sent it love . . .
And a miracle happened!

Within a week, my tree self grew five tiny shoots,
    which soon became five smooth, young trunks,
    and my tree self
        (nurtured by the daily dose of love
            from my human self)
    grew fast into a graceful spreading tree.

When it had grown enough leaves
    to photosynthesise enough sunshine,
    it discarded three of its trunks,
    while the other two sprang high into the sky.
Now, at this moment in our 'pretend time',
    there are two slender, white trunks,
    delicately crowned with whispering green leaves.
And the human me-that-I-am-now,
    returning from its daily run in the park,
    hugs my beautiful tree self-that-was,
    and feels the kinship.

There is a me-that-I-am-to-be,
> evolved fifty thousand years from now, and more
>> (in our pretend time)
> which looks at the human me-that-I-am-now,
> and sends love and encouragement,
> so that I may grow and flourish,
> and become as beautiful as my human self can be.

Sometimes, I feel that future-me
> put its arms around now-me, and hold me.

And I feel the kinship,
> and I am lost in love.

Siamese Twins

This tree, from one base
> two canopies flourish in this place:
> two trunks,
> one tree.

This spirit, you and I,
> two bodies here beneath this sky:
> two hearts,
> one me.

Trivia

Trivia, fears, dreams
    are locked with me inside my brain
    (but mostly trivia.)
I'm enmeshed in trivia:
        trivia — dreams,
            trivia — fears,
                trivia — loneliness.
Trivia, trivia, trivia –
    soporific companions!

I woke from this bad sleep once.
No struggling –
    the brain just evaporated
    and I was free!
Great vistas of Reality engulfed me then
    and I discovered Joy.

So why am I back in here now,
    crammed into this cloying morass
    inside my brain
    where peace eludes me?

Must I wait for Death
    to help me find Myself again
    – or will that little door
        open for me once more?

An Arcane Adventure

It is the ninth of August 1978,
    and this is the most euphoric awakening I can remember.
I am in my own bed,
    and it feels the most comfortable bed I've ever slept in.
Every tiny particle of my body is utterly relaxed.
Each cell is at peace.

Very softly, in the background,
    the radio is playing Berlioz's 'Romeo and Juliet'.
I am drifting, drowning, in peace.

I hear a voice.
I think, 'Perhaps I'm drifting back to sleep again,'
    but I'm so aware –
    of my body, warm and relaxed under the doona,
    of the music,
    and I know I'm conscious.

The voice is audible, yet I can't tell whether it's male or female.
It's calling me, insistently,
    so magnetic I have to respond.
'Yes,' I whisper, 'I'm here.'
I am suffused with excitement –
    something special, something wonderful is happening.

Discovery | Marni

I feel a little dizzy,
> because I've become aware that my body is
> down there,
> and I'm sort of
> up here.

I remember reading about astral travel –
> is that what's happening?

Am I starting an astral journey?
I'm moving higher –
> I know I'm near the ceiling somewhere.

What's going on?
I haven't had an accident,
> I'm not even sick.

But somehow, for whatever reason,
> I've left my body.

So, come on, I tell myself,
> *open your soul's eyes,*
> *and look down at your body on the bed there.*

I — I can't!
Try again, you just need practice.
I try very hard, but my soul's eyes are stuck fast.
Perhaps my soul is blind?

I know I'm here near the ceiling somewhere,
    but I can't look down.
This isn't what the books say at all.
    I feel like a cripple.
Something's gone wrong here.
Now I'm moving even higher,
    through the roof as if it doesn't exist.
Fear grips me.
        I'M DYING!!!
I know I can't be,
    because there's nothing wrong with me,
    but I am.
No!!
I don't want to die yet!

I move inexorably upward.
Fear becomes panic –
    not yet, I'm not ready!
Two of my children are still at school,
    their father's dead.
Too many loose ends –
    let me tie up the loose ends,
        let me get ready, please?
Give me time to get ready!

... and a thought echoes around me:
   'Fool, do you think anyone
   ever feels ready to die?
House cleaned, everything neatly put away?
Body just bathed,
   soul washed and spread out to dry?
Children and friends neatly stacked
   into their correct futures?
Nobody ever feels ready to die,
   but if their time has come
   they must accept.'

And my time has come.
I have no choice but to accept.
So I resign myself.
Somehow the children will have to find their own way.
Someone (a very faint someone)
   will have to clean a house
   that has almost ceased to exist.
The ends hang loose.
The house, and the children, have gone ...

I am moving through space so fast now!

Past a blur of spangled stars,

    I am racing towards

        INFINITE LIGHT.

    — I'm rushing with joy towards the centre of the light.

It is my whole desire.

It is Joy . . . Peace . . .

    Love.

One last memorable thought:

    'If this is what it's like to die,

        no-one need ever be afraid of death.

    It's wonderful!'

Somewhere before me, around me now, is Light –

    brilliant, so beautiful I cannot resist it.

I am drawn towards it,

    magnetised by its beauty.

It is everywhere, I am aware of nothing but Light,

    and somehow, the source of that Light is love.

Oh, there's no fear now,

    just my longing to be part of the Light.

To be a reciprocating part of the love.

I am surprised to become aware of my body again –

    so I'm not dead after all!

I'm enclosed in flesh once more.

        NO!!

I don't want this prison –
    I don't want to drag this heavy Thing around with me.
It is crippling, inhibiting,
    I can't function — it's rotten.
I want to go back to the Light,
    which is Joy and Peace and Love.

Slowly, my awareness changes –
    my body no longer feels heavy.
It becomes so light, so relaxed,
    the flesh feels luxurious.
An unseen teacher is giving me a lesson
    in the best possible way:
    I'm learning from my own experience.

Gradually my awareness is drawn
    to each part of my body in turn.
And as my awareness centres on it,
    that part of my body feels pleasurable,
    beautiful.
My body is a Joy –
    the blood is singing happy songs in my veins.
Everything, it seems, is unfolding naturally
    as a delicious sensuality pervades my body
    and I become a child again,
    innocent in my acceptance of the pleasure it brings.

Child-like
>   (childish?)
>   the thought that springs to my mind
>   is so twee I can't believe it:
>   'My own little pleasure centre,' I think, 'how lovely!'
>> (It's not me — later I squirm at the thought of it.)

I am feeling as if I — this Being –
>   have entered a body for the first time,
>   being given a tour of inspection, so to speak,
>   and I am naive in the wonder of a new discovery.

The lesson is clear:
'This body is My gift to you,
>   don't despise it –
>   it should be a pleasure to you.
Be grateful, and use it well.'

And I am grateful.
Relaxed,
>   euphoric,
>> I lie and luxuriate a little longer.

I won't despise my body any more.
Please, show me how to use it well –
>   show me how to make those I contact
>   glad to have met me.

Later, I can think about it again
> with my worldly adult mind.
I understand the lesson,
> I remember how I felt;
> but in nine years I tell the story
> to three people only.
How could I find the words –
> how could people ever understand?
Now I'm writing it down, because
> maybe, somewhere out there,
> there is someone with the innocent eyes of a child –
> eyes that see purity as something beautiful.
And maybe that person
> can understand my lesson.

Let others cast their crude aspersions,
> of course they will!
But they can't touch
> those of us to whom the lesson is taught.
That part of us goes so deep
> they'll never reach so far.

Now I am content.
I have seen wonders,
> and I know that somehow — in some other dimension –
> such wonders exist.
But I'm grateful for this body.
I came back to it because this is where I should be,
> for now;
> and when the time is right,
> I will find that dimension again.

In the meantime,
    I have other, perhaps more painful lessons to learn.
I want to be a good student –
    after all,
    I'm involved in my subject:
        this thing we call Life.

This happened — it happened to me.

When I set out to record it ten years later, it was simply to help me remember, although the basic experience remains etched in my mind forever.

Although I intended to write about it in prose, just for myself, somehow the poetic form seemed insistent. I've had three major spiritual experiences in my life, all completely different. This was the second — I would say the first ('Enlightenment') was the most profound, but this was more dramatic.

I've chosen the words of this poem very carefully in my attempt to share this experience with you. I hope I've made it clear that while the latter part of the experience was not at all sexual, it was surprisingly and delightfully sensual.

Morning Meditation

Body soft as cotton wool,
    mind a tumble-jumble of thoughts
    like moths flying 'round my head.
Briefly
    one flutters wildly into focus,
        then another:
                'Don't catch them,
                let them fly away.'

Focussed now –
    body heavy,
        tastes,
            smells,
                sounds . . .
                      life energy surging within.

Ignore the circling thoughts –
    see them slowly slip away,
        each dropping one word
                trailing behind it
        . . . like a glowing flare.

Single words,
    sounds echoing in my ears,
        out of context,
    meaning nothing.

From their nothingness
>	a wonderment arises:
>	can you think
>	– can you conceive an idea –
>	without words,
>	without language to capture the meaning?

How else –
>	mental pictures perhaps?

And the language of the soul –
>	is it love?

But my questions are thoughts –
>	so I let them pass.

They drift,
>	words,
>>	moths
>>>	and fire-flies together,
>>>>	fading further
>>>>	and further
>>>>>	. . . into a mist of distance.

Suspended in nothingness
>	– floating –
>	a small, numinous sense of joy
>	begins to grow within my body,
>>	like the sun
>>>	rising in a dark valley:
>>	swelling, flowing,
>>>	suffusing body and mind
>>>	with light.

I gather this light
 – garner this joy –
  in my morning meditation.
I will carry it
  throughout the day,
  for without it
    I am nothing.

Play of Fear

Fear has reached out,
    wrapped icy fingers
    around my chest.
Something in my throat
    has tightened into a hard knot.

God — I can't swallow!

I open my mouth
    trying to relax my jaw,
    but strands of the knot
    are pulled too tight.

My mouth is so dry –
    tongue a lump of wood
    rattling inside a hollow drum.
Now my left leg's begun to shake –
    I can't control it!
I reach out to steady myself,
    grasp hold of a piece of scenery.

Surely the audience is wondering
> about this thunderous noise
> emanating from my chest?

The stage-manager looks up
> from his lighted desk –
> just checking I'm ready for my cue.

Can't he hear my heartbeat?
It's so loud I can barely hear the dialogue!
No — he smiles,
> flicks me a devil-may-care wink.

Can't he see I'm dying
> here in the wings?

The drum in my chest
> is beating too fast,
> racing,
>> racing –
>>> it's running away with me!

I draw in huge gulps of air,
> expanding my chest,
> stilling my heart.

Snatches of dialogue filter through the drumming.
The actors look as if
> they're enjoying being out there,
> the audience roaring with laughter.

They're certainly enjoying it.

Now –
    here comes my cue!
Will these stiff legs
    carry me on stage?
Will this dry mouth work?

As I move into the bright light,
    my character's personality
        drifts,
     draping itself over me
     like a cloak.
The lines come easily now.
I feel at home
    here on stage.

I am almost completely my character
    – but not quite:
        Watch you don't knock
            that glass of water
            as you move
            between the desk and sofa.
        Remember not to upstage Robert
            on the next line,
                and
            keep out of the shadow
            up stage left.

From the black velvet void
>	beyond the footlights,
>		I hear the audience gasping with laughter –
>			they're right with us.
A wave of sheer pleasure washes over us
>	enfolding cast and audience in its embrace;
>	and in this delicious warmth
>	we revel in our togetherness.

~

At interval the curtain drops
>	with a soft thud.
We walk off stage in little groups:
>	"That went well, didn't it?"
>	'Yes, but Martin nearly forgot
>	to pass me the envelope,
>	did you notice?
>	Thank God he remembered!'

I wander to the dressing room
>	and a longed-for cup of tea.
>	This is fun –
>	I love this job!

Two-Way Mirror

It has gone full circle:
    the little girl,
      once scolded for being naughty,
      now scolds the mother for being old.

It works both ways:
    when you look with love,
    you find yourself understanding;
        and
    when you understand,
    you find yourself loving.

Who do you see in the two-way mirror?
    Do you see the refugees?

        Can you see the refugees?

Daniel was my son's first baby and the source of much wonder.

See Ya!

I watch as he opens his eyes,
    looking at me gently,
    still dreaming of paradise –
    all pink-cheeked, blue-eyed beauty,
    wrapped in a blanket of peace.

The car is moving smoothly through the suburbs,
    as a tiny hand reaches,
    slowly exploring,
    to touch my mouth
    as if it were a thing of wonder.
What is it I see in his eyes –
    acceptance, recognition?

Now his hand curls round my finger,
    not tightly, just making contact.
It feels like a caress, this connection:
    his peace and mine,
    like two drops of water fusing;
    his aura enfolding us both
    in an oasis of peace.

When I leave the car, I say 'Bye-bye,'
    but he doesn't respond;
        just calmly observes my departure.
A few minutes later though, when I return,
    his mother says,
        "He cried when you got out."

So I remember, when I finally depart,
    to say the magic words:
            'See ya!'
And two little hands wave simultaneously,
    the small fingers curling and uncurling.

'Good-bye Daniel,
        See ya!'

The Key to the Theory of Everything

A naïve rumination

String physics, the scientists tell us,
      could hold the key
      to the theory of everything . . .

Wow — eleven dimensions –
      and we're stuck in the first four!

I can go backwards and forwards in space,
    but I can only go forwards in time.
I'm not really competent
    in the fourth dimension yet.
My grandmother was, before she died.
She really lived in the past
    when she was a hundred years old.

Maybe our real selves
    can move about freely in all dimensions;
    only we're stuck here
    because our vibrations are too slow
    to take us beyond the fourth.

And maybe it's when our higher selves
> drop down to this level, that we have
> those wonderful flashes of illumination.

And then, when our vibrations speed up,
> we go off to explore the higher dimensions,
> and leave the slow, heavy body part behind –
> like my grandmother did.

And that's death.

But if we're silly enough to die
> *before* our vibrations speed up,
> we have to create ourselves another body
> to keep us going down here,
> just until our vibrations get revved up enough
> to take us into the next dimension.

And that's reincarnation.

I wonder if there's something in this string physics thing after all,
> and those tiny strings
> really do contain the answer to everything?

Wish I was a scientist!

Now

In the pale light of dawn
    I stand before the shining mirror
of the Lake of Time,
        stoop,
and gently extend my hand
to trail a finger through the quiet water.

In silent wonder
    I gaze at the drop of water left
gleaming on my finger tip,
seeing there
all the qualities of that mysterious lake.

No small part of what once was
    has ever drowned beneath the flood
of Now and yet to come;
        but
in each drop lies all we ever were,
all we have yet to be.

We parted before we met,
    and if we ever loved
we still love now.

Beyond the Biological Computer

Beyond all the complexity,
    it's really so simple.

I used to say
    the brain's a limiting factor,
    but it seemed no-one agreed with me.
Then one night on TV
    I heard Krishnamurti say
    "The brain is the enemy of the soul,"
        and I heaved a great sigh of relief:
At last — a fellow traveller!

I've always felt
    the brain restricts us
    within its suffocating parameters.
That when we dare to go
    beyond all the scientific probing,
        beyond intellectual analysing
            – when we're free of the
            biological computer in our heads –
                then

Discovery | Marni

    I can imagine us expanding
        with a sigh of relief,
        as we find our place
        beyond all the complexity
            where
    it's all so simple.

Now we see as in a glass darkly, but then face to face   (St Paul)

City Streets

People are hiding behind their eyes
    – peeping out –
    shyly, some of them,
    while others glare,
    daring you to criticise.

Some feign indifference,
    pretending they don't care.
Their attitude suggests
    you're not really there.
People hiding behind their eyes
    make you wonder
        is anyone there?
    Blank looks,
            lost in a stare . . .

But behind those eyes is the real man
    – peeping out.
It's lonely and frightening
    hiding in there,
    and really he's longing
    for someone to care.

Reach out with your eyes –
    let him see that you're there!

Discovery | Marni

I toured Australia back in 1973 with the J.C. Williamson theatre company. At the end of our Adelaide season, while the company flew the cast to Perth, the scenery and props were to travel across the continent by road. This meant a wait of almost a week before our season could open there. Having secured accommodation, I decided to take a bus to Albany on the south coast, and spend a few days with an old school friend.

It was a long journey and the bus was crowded, so I was very grateful to the elderly gentleman who offered his seat to me — an Aboriginal man with grizzled hair, neatly dressed in a clean suit and open-neck shirt. He stood for the rest of the journey, but got off a few stops before Albany. When he left the bus, the few remaining passengers began talking loudly and derisively about the Aboriginal 'problem'. I sat squirming, wishing I could think of something arresting to say that would make them stop and think. I've always been sorry that my brain failed me on that occasion.

A few years later, I saw a film titled *Munda Nyuringu*. It was more of a documentary really, and its content re-ignited my anger to such an extent that I felt I had to write this poem to get it out of my system.

Munda Nyuringu

(An open letter to the ABC, 1986.)

Written in the white heat of anger after seeing the documentary Munda Nyuringu in 1986

I remember when I was a kid,
    at school and at Sunday school,
    they used to tell us about slavery –
    which always occurred in other countries, of course.

They'd tell us how evil it was,
    and talk about Wilberforce
    and all the other guys who fought so hard
    to stamp it out.
"Of course it's all gone now," they'd say;
    suggesting that we're living
    in a more enlightened age these days.

    Oh yeah?
That was pre-1945!
Now they tell me . . .

Know what?
Right while we were having those lessons,
    Aborigines were in neck chains in WA!

Well, we weren't to know, were we,
    safely tucked away here in Victoria?
Mind you, our own mob down at Lake Tyers
    was kept like prisoners;
    and we couldn't know that either,
    because visitors weren't allowed in –
    well, not without a 'special permit' that is,
    just in case the truth got out!

More recently in WA
    the community wanted this Aboriginal blot on the landscape
    hidden away — out of sight, out of mind.
So they gave them a tract of land –
    well away from town, of course.
Big deal!
    I mean it wasn't any use for anything else.
And they built them shanties there too.
No walls, mind you –
    just a bit of a roof, and a couple of supports.
Well, that's all the Abos want, isn't it?
    And it's cheaper.

So when it's cold, they try to sleep in their cars,
    and they look shabby and demoralised.

They tell us that back in the early days,
> when the first contact with so-called civilisation occurred,
> the Abos were a proud, happy, generous people.

So what happened?
> – we did!

Listen Whitey, if you don't like the way the Abos live,
> you don't have to.

They've lost their roots, some of them,
> or their dreaming.

But wise up to this fact:
> it's because of the way they've been treated
>> by the likes of you.

Not until we all feel shame enough to make those blokes in Canberra
> – oh, sorry, *persons* in Canberra –
> not until we make them aware that
> these are people we want respected,
> only then should they cease showing this film.

And every complacent, self-satisfied big shot
> who thinks he's better
> (instead of just luckier)
> should be clapped in irons
> and forced to watch it.

> So how about it, ABC?
> Start the trend . . .
>> eh?

Fellow Traveller

She was riding the City Circle, I think –
    it soon became clear that she had no home.
She boarded the train shaking
    and sat in a heap,
        an almost empty cloth bag on her lap.
She looked to be in her late thirties, maybe forty,
    every second tooth missing.

From the bag she took a phone and an open exercise book,
    names and numbers scrawled on every line,
    most of them scored out.
She rang the next number on the list.
Her voice breaking — a mix of desperation and fear –
    she asked for a room.
"I've been sleeping behind the primary school in Elwood," she said.
    "I haven't eaten since Friday."

She put the phone down, sobbing.
The man next to me handed her a tissue.
She said thanks.
I opened my purse (out of sight in my bag)
    and my hand clasped a twenty dollar note.
I remembered my self-admonition:
    'This must last a fortnight,
        no impulse buys,   I must pay off my credit card.'
She sat opposite me, a bundle of despair and misery,
    perhaps gathering strength to make the request.

Then she leaned forward to ask timidly,
    "Do you have any change you could spare?"
The man beside me left the train.
I thought, 'I get off at the next stop,
    I'll give her the note as I leave.'

She went on: "Most places charge eighty dollars,
    but I've found one that charges forty.
They're holding it for me till tonight,
    but I haven't got any money."
I asked about Centrelink.
"I've applied," she said,
    "but you have to wait two weeks — till Wednesday."
Salvation Army?
"They told me their funds are frozen till Wednesday."

I placed the twenty dollar note on her lap,
    noticing as I did so the messy hair,
    the rank smell –
    she hadn't showered since long before Friday!
There are con artists among Melbourne's homeless –
    she was clearly not one of them.
What was it like behind that school, I wondered.
Suddenly the nights had become very cold,
    she wore only slacks and a jumper.
Had she perhaps even been threatened
    lying there alone in the freezing dark?

Discovery | Marni

She stared at the note, uncomprehending.
It lay on her lap untouched.
I said, 'Put it in your bag before it blows away.
    Maybe you could ring and tell them you've got half,
        and could they wait for the rest till Wednesday?'
She nodded and I patted her leg as I left,
    Whispered, 'Good luck.'

Later I realised it was Monday –
    Tuesday was Budget night.
Everyone, it seems, even the Salvation Army,
    has to freeze their funds till Wednesday.

Later still I thought, there had been a fifty dollar note
    beneath the twenty I gave her.
Why didn't I give her that?

Passacaglia
Spotlight Centre Stage

The sounds of life are blended
    into a continuous hum:
        cars, trucks, bells,
        distant slam of a door
    merge into an ostinato.
Over this weaves the ebb and flow
    of the melody of life:
        the cry of a child,
        the sharp, quick buzz of a passing motorbike . . .
    Somebody dropped something!
It is the hum of life,
    the sound of the world turning.

When I sit on my back porch
    sounds,
        sifted and filtered
        by trees in the park,
    form a muted backdrop
    to my own life,
    played centre stage.

Discovery | Marni

    Close to hand, in the wings,
        I hear the flutter and rustle of a bird in a nearby bush,
        the sigh of wind in the leaves,
            a bird call,
        the hum of an insect.

    While deep inside my head,
        I hear the regular *thump! thump! thump!*
        of my beating heart.
    And in slower rhythm,
        the swish-of-brushes-on-drums sound
        of my lungs filling and emptying –
        the ground bass surge of blood
        singing in my veins.
    The passacaglia of life.

    I am not this body,
        but the music and movement of the life within
        hold the spotlight.

    Passacaglia: a slow instrumental piece characterised by a series of variations on a particular theme played over a repeated bass part.

Moonlight

The moon is a gleaming iridescent pearl
    floating serenely
    in a sea of deep grey satin.
I watch its translucent beams
    caress everything before me
    with enchantment.

In my mind I know
    it merely mirrors the sun's light, but
    it seems luminous.

In my heart I sense
    a loving intelligence surrounding me,
    and feel a strange longing
    to reflect its glow.

Surely, if the hard barren surface of the moon
    can be so simply transformed,
    I too, may share my own soft beauty
    as I float through this sea of darkness.

Is it possible that the translucent beams
    of my reflected light
    could shine on those around me,
    enfolding them in its gentle glow,
    caressing them with enchantment?

So may we all continue reflecting
    and reflecting,
caressing
    and enfolding,
waxing
    and waning,
as our nearness to the Source
    drifts
  . . . further and closer
on our journey through this life!

Until, at last, all is One,
    and I am one with all,
    and this sea of darkness
        is lost in the light.

Camping with Rambo

Their car throbs
    like it's ready to burst.
Young bucks,
        raunchy,
    egos flapping 'round them
    like red tornadoes,
    radios blaring heavy metal.
Look at me — notice ME!
    I'm Rambo!
    I'm Macho!
        See?

Their noise splinters the air like glass –
    cuts through the quiet serenity of my little tent
    dreaming in the shade of the willow trees.

Peacocks strutting in front of the peahen,
    their gaudy tee shirts shriek ugly crudities
    as they flaunt their aggressive masculinity
    in front of every passing, gum-grinding, giggling girl.

Look at me man!
    Like, Wow!

Discovery | Marni

The campground was shrouded in peace before they came,
    air soothed by ambient music
    from the softly gurgling river.
Huge trees casting gentle shade,
    children carrying Li-los
    laughed and played
    as hot sun seared their skin,
    their happy descant floating
    over the floppy smack of mattresses in water.
Grown-ups dozed over books,
    cool drinks in their hands.

    Now!
– their car throbs like it's ready to burst.
Look at me man!
      Like, Wow!

. . . and everyone in the camp ground knows
      Rambo rides again!

Back in the 1970s, when the ABC first gave us the opportunity to view David Attenborough's *Life of Animals*, I was enthralled by his vision of African exotica, but less than excited when it was announced that the following week's episode would feature the garden snail. I knew exactly what they would do: put the camera under a sheet of glass and show us all the slimy secret underpinnings as a snail glided across my widescreen TV. In spite of misgivings, I switched it on and, needless to say, I was once again fascinated.

With amazing synchronicity the following morning, when I went down the front steps to get the mail, there were two of them, right on the next step, engaged in sexual congress. As a gardener I knew exactly what I should do, but somehow I couldn't. I checked an hour or so later and they were still fully involved — the act literally proceeded at a snail's pace — and my mind kept saying 'squash them', as I envisaged my garden crawling (or should I say slithering?) with the creatures. Of course the next time I looked they'd left, without even a snail trail…

On the Dual Sexuality of the Common Garden Snail

Mr and Mrs Gastropod Mollusc Hellicidae
    had a son they called Helix Aspersa.
They were very proud of him
    (he was such a good boy)
    and they never felt tempted to curse her.

So let's sing a song of praise
    to clever young Helix,
    who never had to worry
    if his friend was Sue or Felix,
    and who didn't have to check if his friend wore pink or blue,
    'cause any other snail would do.

Mr and Mrs Gastropod Mollusc Hellicidae
    had a life that was free of fear.
They didn't have to worry if their son was bisexual,
    or care if he seemed to be queer.
They knew he'd never suffer an identity crisis –
    their future was bright and clear.

So let's sing a song of praise
    to clever young Helix,
    who didn't have to worry
    if his friend was Sue of Felix,
    and who really didn't care if his friend wore pink or blue,
    'cause any other snail would do.

Mr. and Mrs. Gastropod Mollusc Hellicidae
    had a son who was unlike any other.
Their bosoms swelled with pride
    when one day he came inside,
    and told them, "I'm going to be a mother!"

So let's sing a song of praise
    to clever young Helix,
    who never had to worry
    if his friend was Sue or Felix
    and who didn't give a damn if his friend wore pink or blue,
    'cause any old snail would do.

The Hellicidaes glowed with transparent joy
    over the accomplishments of their boy.
But the question inherent in a tale like this is:
    which one was Mr,
        and which was Mrs?

The Gardener

for Margaret

She's a Taurean, you see,
    and the love of gardens
    is instinctive in her heart.

When I took her
    to the local farmers market recently,
    she bought a bare-rooted rose bush.

'Where will you put it?' I gasped.
I don't think she was too sure herself,
    because she lives in an upstairs flat.

But last time I visited her
    there it was on the balcony
    with all the multitude of other plants
    she'd never been able to resist.

Soon she'll abandon sitting there in the sun,
    the chair overgrown by jungle.
She'll just sidle carefully between the pots
    to water her babies.
Well, she's a Taurean, you see,
    and her love of gardens
        is instinctive.

        Margaret assures me that this will NEVER happen.

Walking the Desert

"Little rivulets of sound came
      to accentuate
      the silence of the desert."
The man on the radio
      is talking about his walk
      in the desert at night.

His voice echoes in my mind:
      "Little rivulets of sound
      to accentuate the silence."

I imagine silence:
      palpable,
      almost solid.
Pierced –
      a creature stirring,
          then silence,
      a breeze whispering in my ears,
          silence,
      feet soft on shifting sands.
          Silence.

And I remember long ago, sitting
    immersed in the glory of my epiphany
        – vibrant –
    as little rivulets of self began to intrude
    to accentuate the Oneness.

Now the process is reversed:
    immersed in the world once more,
    little rivulets of Infinite Oneness
    filter in to my soul,
        to accentuate
    the separateness of Creation.

Moonshine Magic

Breathe the magic,
    feel it seep
    slowly into your soul . . .

It was after midnight, you see,
    when I drew the curtains,
    and moonbeams beckoned me
    into the garden.

Out here, a near-full moon
    calmly weaves its spell
    from a clear, translucent sky.

Inky shadows pattern
    soft veils of light,
    as they spread themselves
    across a lawn gleaming
    with the diamonds of recent rain.

Garden table and chairs shimmer,
    and the gum tree,
    – black lace flung
    across an opalescent sky –
    is spangled with a myriad blazing stars.

The night is hushed,
    accepting, expectant.
All of nature, it seems,
    is sensing the magic;
        and
    I am standing in it,
    breathing it,
        feeling the magic seep
        slowly into my soul.

Metaphors and Mysteries

as in the macrocosm, so in the microcosm

1

I often wonder whether God speaks to us in metaphors –
    "Phase proportionate,"
    as the psychologist would say,
    to our ability to understand . . .

Planets whirl around their suns
    while atoms spin around the nucleus,
    all caught in a web of magnetic attraction –
        and we?

In the turbulence of youth
    we're caught too –
        butterflies, trapped in a web
        of mystery and longing;
        the fine threads of attraction drifting
        like an invisible cobweb,
        holding us enmeshed.

Yet ultimately,
> from the ecstasy of our union,
> arises our most beautiful act of creation.

Like butterflies too, we flutter through life
> never seeing the threads of Spirit
> drawing us with unspoken longing
> for our Spiritual Lover.

So our yearning to be one with all that is
> remains unrecognised,
>> unarticulated;
>>> only the pain real,
>>>> and the separation,
>>>>> and the alone-ness.

I wonder:
> when those spiritual threads finally
> draw us into union of the spirit,
> will it bring deeper fulfilment
> than we could ever know
> in this dimension of experience?

And will that transcendent fulfilment
> spark the creation of something as yet unimaginable
>> – something glowing with life
>> and pure potential?

2

I wonder too:

Are we, even now,
    embryos,
        living in the womb of the world?

Is death a cosmic contraction
    forcing us
        – too often painfully
        but sometimes peacefully –
    through the spiritual birth canal?

Our weakness in death perhaps,
    is but the weakness of a baby
    thrust eventually into the light,
    and arriving,
        – at last –
    into the nurturing and love
    of the Real Life beyond.

Could it be
    that when our time has finally come,
    we hear a distant call
    drawing us home
        (our spiritual parents perhaps –
        or our spiritual lover?)
Maybe, in the end,
        we go with joy
                to meet our Beginning!

3

Sometimes I do feel like an embryo
    living in the womb of the world.
I can almost feel the strong, thick umbilical cord
    pulsing with energy;
    bringing me healing,
        strength,
            vitality;
    my spirit mother surrounding me
    with her protection and nourishment.

I sense,
    as long as I stay open to her energy,
    this pulsating bond
    will keep me strong and healthy.

But I wonder:
    as I draw closer
    to my birthing time,
    could the cord shrivel,
    and I die stillborn?
Must I draw consciously
    on this invisible sustenance? . . .

So that if I choose,
    I will pass healthy
    through the jaws of death
    – now the spiritual pelvic bones –
    opening peacefully,
    as I am delivered into new Life?

As a new-born spirit baby
    will there be a spirit mother
    to nurture me –
    guiding my eagerness
    to explore this new Reality?

    . . . until perhaps
    I grow and develop
    into my true spiritual inheritance!

And then?

Sometimes I have little intuitive wonderings
    whether I may then discover
        I am my own mother.

4

My little life gone,
    its concerns dropped away
    like dust blowing in the autumn breeze.
Metaphors hold no meaning now,
    mysteries no longer intrigue.

I am everywhere at once
    – and nowhere,
    for I am one with everything,
    known and knowing.

Bliss so penetrating
    I am lost in it.

Delphic Oracle

"*Know yourself,*"
    says the Delphic Oracle,
        "*for therein lies your Heaven*
        and your Hell."

Ties loosen.
As soul and body part,
    the journey begins;
        passing through the tunnel
        that leads to light.

Leads not outward and upward
    toward some mystical heaven –
        this tunnel leads to
        the Light within.

Those flashes of light and insight
    that thrilled you –
    remember?
Those moments of fear and despair
    that chilled you –
            where are they?

All comes from the Self,
    and now you journey
    into what You are:
        beyond your intellect
        and your mental potential,
        for you and your brain
        have parted company now.

Shorn of the mask of personality
    you travel now to your intrinsic joy
        and warmth
        and love;
Robed in your capacity
    to be entranced
        or to be bored,
    to know fear
        or peace.

"Know Yourself,"
    thunders the Delphic Oracle,
        "for this *becomes* your Heaven
            – or your Hell!"

Light

I tried to pick up a piece of light.
There in the dark cupboard,
    I thought a piece of peel had fallen
    from the compost bin;
    but my fingers closed over –
    nothing.

I tried to pick up a piece of light,
    but found myself
    still there in my mundane life
    with the compost bin
    and the dishes,
    and the laundry piled with washing.
Light doesn't work that way.

Once, years ago now,
    I left my body and went to the light.
It brought a rush of absolute joy
    and blissful freedom.
I thought
    I'll carry this light with me always
    on my life-path.

And now, here I am
    surrounded by my mundane life,
    with compost bin
    and dishes
    and the laundry piled with washing.

I can't carry that light with me
    hidden in my pocket,
    or even in my heart.
I must take my mundane life to the light
    so that both my life and I
    can absorb it's radiance.
And then, perhaps,
        we both may shine.

Linked Haiku

An egg lies at rest
in a nest of soft dry grass,
smooth brown shell shining.

This strong, fragile shell
cradles a living treasure
waiting to be born.

The newly hatched chick
flounders, struggling to survive –
one day it will fly!

Your false persona –
when shattered like an eggshell,
miracles emerge!

C.G Jung suggests that the personality we project
can be at great variance to the authentic self.

Dreams

for Lance

Your mind is full of dreams . . .
You dream of flying:
>   mentally you check your hang-glider,
>> sense the wind,
>>> perch yourself on a cliff edge,
>>>> and step off.

The sensation — the peace — of floating aloft
>   is something you endlessly long for.

You fill your room with books on flight,
>   magazines about flight,
>   and in your mind you constantly practise the techniques.

But I think the act of flying
>   is only a small part of your dreams.

You long, I think,
>   to step off the edge of your busy life,
>   to leave all the petty concerns and worries behind.

To float and soar –
>   live in the joy of the motion,
>   the joy of the moment.

To forget that anything exists below.

Discovery | Marni

It's no longer possible to live the simple life –
    no matter where you go,
        the government wants details for its taxes,
        and the council's after you for rates which,
            'if not paid on or before the appropriate date
            will bear interest from the day on which
            they became payable at the rate of interest
            as provided for in section 366
            of the Local Government Act.'

So many petty laws and by-laws to be observed,
    so much red tape!
Bureaucracy has driven the simple life
    out the metaphorical window.
Your spare time's not spare any more,
    it's spent on maintenance,
        repairs
            shopping
                paperwork
                    mowing lawns!
There's no time left to find yourself.

Dreams

So you mentally perch on the edge,
    take off,
        and float into nothingness . . .
            swooping and soaring in sheer pleasure,
                with never a memory,
                      never a plan.
No doubt one day they'll find a way
    to invade our dreams
    and tax them, too.
Until then, dream your dreams my love,
    and I'll dream mine.

Daemons

Not my crossroads, but yours,
    this cancer thing.
Health glowed within me
    like a living current.

So . . . it was a shock.
I couldn't quite believe the doctor
    when she told me
      "It's malignant."

You were wonderful then:
    driving me to the surgeon
    who predicted
    "You'll have quite a battle on your hands."

But I didn't.
My intuition proved right, only
    we weren't to know that then.

Yes, you *were* wonderful:
> driving me to Warrandyte to purchase
> enchanted ear rings,
> their silver scrolls set with
> amethysts, moonstones
> and fresh water pearls:
> your offering to soothe my uncertain soul.

Then . . . on to a comedy,
> conjuring the trivial
> to banish reality.

Laughter *is* the best medicine.

And next day driving me to hospital,
> saying with vast conviction,
> "We'll fight this together,
> and we'll win!"

That vast conviction evaporated
> faster than mist
> on a summer's morning.

It lasted another day or two,
when you arrived at hospital
> bearing the most enormous card I'd ever seen
>> (get well messages carefully formed
>> by your pupils' wobbly hands),
> I was moved and thrilled —
> for the last time.

Discovery | Marni

After that you left.
Oh not physically,
    just mentally and emotionally.

    Just . . .

For three long, arid years you lingered.
'It's not you, it's me,'
    you replied to my tearful questions,
    'don't worry, I'll get over it.'
You never did.

Over the years I'd seen
    you shun sick people,
    but I was well.
The surgeon had examined every organ,
    and replaced them –
    rather loosely I thought,
    when taking my first morning run,
    everything flopping around inside.

Pathology had reported
    the cancer walled off,
    my body clear.
I was ready to face life!

But at the crossroads
> you had faced your daemons
> and found them so scary
> you changed direction –
> took another path.

So, I continued into life . . .

> Alone.

Discovery | Marni

They Say . . .

They say you shouldn't pick your nose,
      they say you mustn't fart.
They say it's rude to stare at things
      — except for *objets d'art*.

They told me, "Don't take off your clothes
      when swimming in the sea –
      it's awful to expose yourself
      between the neck and knee."

They told me nice girls never flirt.
They said, "Just watch your stance,"
      and
"Always wear a dress or skirt
      – nice girls don't wear pants."

When I was young, that's what they said.
I've tried with all my might
      to understand why
      all these things feel
      natural and right.

The Clay Statuette

A little clay statuette stands on my piano –
    a tall attenuated figure
    elegant in tails,
    one hand turning a page of music,
    a baton in the other . . .

Music, Maestro, please!

I remember how I came by this musical gentleman.
So in love I was then,
    and very afraid to let myself love you completely . . .
    you were so much younger than I.
'Surely,' I told myself, 'The time will come
    when he'll turn to someone younger.'
And I knew I couldn't bear the pain of that.

So I held back.
You swore commitment — remember?
"We're together forever," you said,
    "in this life and the next!"
Of course . . .

But your boyish enthusiasm for our shared adventure in life
    knew no bounds
    and slowly,
    naively perhaps,
    I let myself believe you,
    trust you.

I did know fear
    when you began walking to school with Hilary –
    two young student teachers
    on the way to your first teaching round together.
You'd talked of Hilary often:
    Hilary said this,
    Hilary did that,
    Hilary had a beautiful singing voice.

What's more, she'd pulled strings
    in order to gain a placement
    at the same school as you.
So each morning for two weeks she called for you
    – here at our home –
    and off you went,
    walking through the sunlit park together.

The Clay Statuette

The fear grew huge.
I was cold and numb with it
    the day you came home so late,
        looking smugly pleased with yourself.
"We stopped at a gift shop," you said,
    "because Hilary had to buy a wedding present."
You were flushed with the pleasure of what you'd just done.
"And I bought you this,
    because I knew you'd love it."

So I unwrapped the little man at his podium,
    and you were right –
    I *was* delighted!

You were proud and pleased with yourself
    for having thought of something
    which you knew would bring me so much pleasure.
Penniless,
    putting yourself through teachers college,
    you'd still managed to buy me
    an un-birthday, don't-have-to sort of present.
        A gift of love!

I suppose it was a gift of gratitude too,
    because it was through our sharing
    that you discovered the thrill of classical music,
    embodied now in the elegant gentleman
    I was holding in my hand.

Discovery | Marni

A year or so later when we were playing,
    happy in our togetherness,
    something you said
    – I forget what it was –
    made me laugh,
    and throwing my arms wide,
    'Oh, I love you!' I giggled.
And as I did so,
    one hand knocked my conductor friend
    from his piano podium,
    and aghast, I looked as he lay
    – smashed –
    on the floor.

So patient you were then.
You picked up every tiniest piece,
    and, placing them all in a box,
    you took the box off to your study.
There were so many little pieces,
    I knew he was quite unfixable,
    so I mourned the loss of my clay music master
    – and put him out of my mind.

The Clay Statuette

The fear grew huge.
I was cold and numb with it
    the day you came home so late,
        looking smugly pleased with yourself.
"We stopped at a gift shop," you said,
    "because Hilary had to buy a wedding present."
You were flushed with the pleasure of what you'd just done.
"And I bought you this,
    because I knew you'd love it."

So I unwrapped the little man at his podium,
    and you were right –
    I *was* delighted!

You were proud and pleased with yourself
    for having thought of something
        which you knew would bring me so much pleasure.
Penniless,
    putting yourself through teachers college,
    you'd still managed to buy me
    an un-birthday, don't-have-to sort of present.
        A gift of love!

I suppose it was a gift of gratitude too,
    because it was through our sharing
    that you discovered the thrill of classical music,
    embodied now in the elegant gentleman
    I was holding in my hand.

Discovery | Marni

A year or so later when we were playing,
    happy in our togetherness,
    something you said
    – I forget what it was –
    made me laugh,
    and throwing my arms wide,
    'Oh, I love you!' I giggled.
And as I did so,
    one hand knocked my conductor friend
    from his piano podium,
    and aghast, I looked as he lay
    – smashed –
    on the floor.

So patient you were then.
You picked up every tiniest piece,
    and, placing them all in a box,
    you took the box off to your study.
There were so many little pieces,
    I knew he was quite unfixable,
    so I mourned the loss of my clay music master
    – and put him out of my mind.

You could see my amazement when,
>   some months later,
>   you presented me with my musical friend,
>   looking like new again.

Well, almost . . .

It's true it looks now as though
>   he's ripped the page of music,
>   in his haste to turn it over.

And he'd lost his baton,
>   so now he flourishes a new one
>   which looks suspiciously like a toothpick.

But the nicest thing is what you said
>   when you presented him to me
>   for the second time.

"If anything ever happens," you said,
>   "to destroy our love,
>   I'll just as patiently take the pieces
>   and put them together again."

No wonder I felt so secure in our love!

And eight years later
> almost to the day,
>> you left me for a younger woman . . .

Oh, love!

Are you, after all, just another man?
I always believed you were something more . . .

And my little statuette still stands
> – lonely –
>> on the piano.

In Winter in Mallacoota

"Mallacoota will always mean Marni to me," you said,
    "I could never take anyone else there."
That was a little over half a year ago,
    and never is over already.
Today you took her –
    to the honeymoon cabin where we shared so much
    four years ago.

It lives in my mind, still with its little brass Indian lamps
    set with coloured glass
    casting soft rainbows of colour through the cosy room,
    the antique pot belly stove creating an oasis of warmth
    in the crisp night air,
    the brilliant stars outside, and . . .
        Oh! It's a full moon!
Yes, I remember how the moon spreads sheets of sparkling silver
    across the lake.

Discovery | Marni

Inside, light from the lamp over the dining table
    spills through the window
    and lights possums eating, fighting and playing
    on their feeding table — really the huge window sill.
I remember how we stood there, naked in the pot-bellied warmth,
    watching the possum mother with her baby.
And I know that in the morning you will pull back the curtains,
    and winter sun will flood the room
    as it always does in July, in Mallacoota.
You will throw back the covers on the huge bed
    and lie naked — as we did –
    sunbathing in the winter sunshine.
Ah, the slow drowsy warmth
    of the mixture of sun and love and peace
    on that soft, soft bed!

And as you breakfast on toast and fruit,
    and drink herb tea,
    the possum feeding table will have transformed
    into a bird feeding table.
There will be rosellas and rainbow lorikeets,
    and you will hear the music of the magpies.

And then by day you will take her,
    eager to delight her,
    and show her all the special places
    we discovered together.

You will climb Genoa Peak
    and see the splendour of the lakes,
    and the sea,
    and wave after wave of mountain ranges
    rippling around you.
(Will the swifts still be darting and swirling
    in the mountain magic?)
And you will clamber around the rocks at Genoa Falls,
    and re-discover our secret beaches,
    and eat Marge's Magic Meals.

And then, tired and happy,
    you will retire to the intimate warmth
    of the pot belly,
    and your books,
    and your special music,
    and the possums,
    and the big, soft bed,
    and the morning sunshine.

Discovery | Marni

Will you tell her how we camped there once,
    and when we returned
        – too late –
    from the other side of the lake,
    a freak swell bottled the yacht
    and dumped us and our belongings in the water?
And how, returning after dark wet and frozen,
    we showered; and then,
    as we cooked dinner in our tent
        (at ten thirty at night)
    the gas bottle ran out;
    so we had to run the half-cooked meal
    and all the extra ingredients
    up to the public barbecue,
    and finish cooking in the cold dark wind by the lake?

Perhaps you will.

And will you tell her how we made love in the sunlight
    at the foot of the cliff on our secret beach?
No, you won't tell her that!
Will you remember?

When our holiday came to an end,
    we were already eager to find

our peaceful intimacy once again;
so we made another reservation
years in advance –
everyone wants the honeymoon cabin!

And as we grew tired and jaded
    with the rush and tension of our life in the city
        (our life of timetables and deadlines
        and excitement
        and stimulation)
    as we grew tired and jaded,
    I waited for the blessing of renewal
    I knew awaited us there.

Four years I waited,
    and today you took her instead.
"I could never take anyone else there," you said,
    half a year ago.

I am in danger of surrendering to despair:
    am I a fool to expect people
    to be true to what they say?
Is that asking too much perhaps?
    because
    then they'd have to *know*
    what they're saying!

Guru

Do not feel guilty for leaving me, my love –
    the pain of my aloneness,
    the pain of my weakness,
    sent me searching
    through the shards of my shattered being
    to find a Me
    I didn't know existed.

Never would I have found
    my strength and self-sufficiency
    cocooned as I was
    within the cotton-wool warmth of our love.

Now I look at the shape of my life
    and understand:
        We needed to be together –
            we taught each other so much.
        And we needed to part
            in order to find
            the hidden Teacher within.

Do not feel guilty for leaving me –
    the pain was part of the Teaching . . .

Cronesong

I think I need a new walking stick –
    this one throws me off-balance
    and makes me limp.
I need an upgrade.

I think I need a new mirror –
    this one shows me a face
    I don't much like
I need a new model.

I think I need a new brain –
    this one's too slow
    and makes mistakes.
I need a recharge.

I think I need a new me –
    this isn't what I want to be,
       – and –
    your expectations won't let me be
    the wiser, warmer, wittier me
    that I wish you could see.

When I Was Young . . .

When I was young
    there was music . . .
Sometimes my heart
    would leap with the joy of it,
    and my soul would sing.
It seemed then
    my whole being was encompassed
    with the glory of the music
            . . . when I was young.

When I was young
    there was laughter . . .
Sometimes the silliest thing
    would draw it
    from wells of happiness deep within.
It seemed then
    my whole being was
    laughing for the sheer joy living.
            . . . when I was young.

When I was young
> there was beauty . . .

Sometimes my heart
> would melt with the excruciating loveliness
> hidden even within ugliness.

It seemed then
> the whole of creation was an expression
> of the beauty living within us all.
>> . . . when I was young.

When I was young
> there was love . . .

Sometimes my heart would overflow,
> nestling as it did
> within the warmth
> of love surrounding it.

It seemed then
> that beyond circumstances,
> beyond people,
> the universe around me
> was simply love.
>> . . . when I was young.

And now –
    what is ageing but a process,
    a letting go?
Allowing your soul to begin
    its drift through the molecules of the universe.

Allowing yourself
    to become once more
    the music
        the laughter,
            the beauty
                and the love that you truly are.
Second childhood they call it.

When I am old enough
    to be young again,
        I shall be whole.

Peripeteia

(youth's psychological roller-coaster)

Not so much astride two worlds
    as teetering between them;
    neither fully involved
    in the physical world
    nor the spiritual.
Balanced on a knife-edge.
	Not so much astride two worlds
	    as filtering between them;
	    both fully involved
	    in the physical world,
	    and vibrating with the spiritual.
	Flowing through the interface.

In this unreal place
    I could topple
    into a vacuum
    and dissolve into nothingness.
Where is God?
	In this vital space
	    I could be filled
	    with the pure joy of being
	    and dissolve into Truth.
	Part of God!

Confumony

From confusion to harmony with Quantum Physics

Intricate turbulence of tumbling energies,
    conflicting and colliding within itself,
    careering around the cosmos,
    swooping, swivelling, swirling around me:
    this is chaos.
It's a chaos of energy soup out there
    Deepak Chopra tells us.

And within the chaos
    – the very essence of the chaos –
    vibrates a non-material, loving intelligence
    some people choose to call God.

Within me too, this same chaotic soup
    is churning wildly,
    its energies tumbling and colliding,
    skewed with conflicting impulses,
    urges and emotions.

And hidden within my own internal chaos
    vibrates an essence
    – not of this body –
    an essence of love and wisdom
    some people choose to call Soul.

When this fine essence within myself
    recognises its image
    within the chaos around me,
    confusion becomes harmony.

Herein lies strength . . .
Herein lie miracles.

Herein lies . . . God?

In the Arms of Thanatos

(the experience of the process of dying)

Body dissolving with age,   I still feel.

Ears deaf,
    hearing aids abandoned,   I hear music.

My soul is a lake of love,
    waters lapping
    the shores of life.

    A butterfly
        drifts to a flower
        sips and dreams
        remembering fat grub crawling.
    It has transcended that incarnation.
    Strange,
        how easy the change!

    Her dewy home disturbed,
        the spider trembles
        and rears ready to bite.

Sun is a star drawn close.

How close –

    will I dissolve in its centre?

I am hiding in the rainbow,

    falling with the rain,

    I am a rock,

        a tree,

            a bird.

                I AM!

Thanatos: the Greek personification of Death.
Also the term chosen by Freud to indicate the universal death instinct.

Being Myself

"Watch your two hands at work,"
    they told us at the School of Philosophy.
So I watched.
"We'll ask about your experience," they said,
    but they never did.
So I went on watching
        nearly forty years ago.

I still watch — not all the time of course:
    when I'm working quietly
        I watch my hands,
        see the body's movements.
I'm watching my body
    from inside and outside these days.

Experiencing being inside my body
    and watching it from outside,
    experiencing being Myself.

Maybe just experiencing *being* . . .

Recognition

A brief encounter

Needing to reach the top level of the shopping centre,
    I trust myself to the travellator.
But now, here I am at the next level
    facing an escalator,
        and my sense of balance has gone on leave.

I watch the steps unfolding, feel the moving handgrip
    – too fast!
Visions of my top half being hauled away
    before my legs are ready to follow.

"Want some help?"
He's good looking in a stylish, relaxed sort of way,
    dressed in a stylish relaxed sort of way,
    but far too young for me —
        by about sixty years!

'Not many good looking young men
    want to help old ladies,' I comment.
"It's the way my mother brought me up."
I still hesitate. "Come on," he says,
    "I'll come with you."

'But then I'll have to come down again,' I say,
    'and you won't be there — there should be some lifts somewhere.'
He does a quick reconnoitre —
"Down the end," he says, "there are lifts on the right."

As I thank him I ask,
    'What's this you've got written on you?'
Ladies in their late eighties
    don't have a natural affinity for tattoos,
    but it doesn't seem to matter.

It looks like half a tiny necklace
    part-way round his neck:
    beautiful cursive writing, too small for me to read.

"*Respect existence,*" he translates,
    "*or expect resistance.*"

One second to take in the full import —
    'That's *good*'
        and we smile recognition.

It took all of five minutes, I realise later.
    Why do I feel so good about it? –
        for a brief moment, two cells in the body of God
        have recognised each other.

    I wonder:
Does the cell contain all the potential
    of the whole Being?

What people are hungry for is not love as the world understands it,
    but a deep and intimate sharing of the self with the other.

Lesser Gods

We're biding our time,
    we old ones
    – gestating –
    developing our true selves
    firm and solid.

Fine-tuning them
    ready to be born into the Real World.
Gods in embryo.

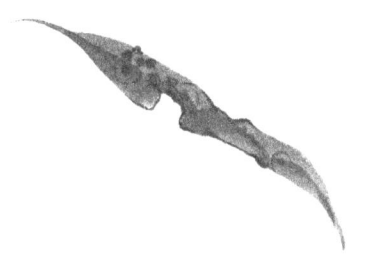

Discovery | Marni

I've been putting off writing this last poem, because I feel so inadequate — there are no words to express this glorious experience in all its intensity, and I fear it will be dismissed as fanciful imaginings.

At the same time, I somehow feel that I must be true to my experience, so I will tell it as it happened. This is where it happened, this is how it happened, this is how I felt:

Luminescence

The Clay Statuette — the aftermath, years later:

The alone-ness is withering my soul.
On the phone at work I wonder
 does the end-of-the-line hear
 as I choke back the sobs?
I try to meditate, but my mind is agitated,
 my emotions agitated.
I'm all jumbled up, and
 peace eludes me.

I try once again.
A whole bleak future stretches before me
 as I sit on the back porch, facing the bush park.
This is a place of peace —
 pot plants explore the slate floor,
 while others tumble from hanging baskets
  (a scrub wren raised her family in one of them last year).

I sit at the wrought iron table and close my eyes,
    reaching once more for that state of mindfulness
  that once came so easily –
      listening as the breeze talks to the treetops while
        birds are socialising,
          distant traffic humming,
            . . . my breathing
              . . . my heartbeat.

There is an energy of peace in the park today,
    that is almost, but not quite tangible.
It comes softly, gently, folding itself around me like a mist,
    yet vibrating with love so potent
    it reaches deep into the centre of my Self.
I'm filled to overflowing — tears running down my face –
      this love,
    so powerful it has me trembling,
      throbbing with emotion,
        entranced.

My whole being is glowing,
    responding to this vibrant energy . . .
      time no longer exists
        my mind no longer exists . . .

But then mind returns, sufficient to ask:
    where does this come from —
    who does it come from?
And a vague remembrance — a teacher once saying,
    'If you ever meet your Guide, ask the name.'

I am afraid to ask,
    I don't want to break the spell —
        eventually, trembling, I venture:
            'Who are you?'
And the answer comes firm and clear:
        'Yourself!'

Now I'm confused — I don't understand.
I get up and move into the house,
    I'm pacing the floor — how can this be?
'You mean my Guide is myself?'
        'Yes!'
I'm both confused and agitated.
I'm being told that my Guide is myself,
    we are the same being.

It feels infinite, this love.
It seems to reach out to me
    from a radiant Being that's not me,
    that is unlike me.

I'm just a useless weak little worm — I know that.
It doesn't make sense —
    I'm trying to understand
        . . . it takes a long time.

    . . . Me — Myself
        . . . and God?
A remembrance from 'Enlightenment' :
'I am me forever
    but that me is inseparably part of You . . .

    . . . and I am one with all creation
    because each one of us
    is a tiny part of You!'

Yes, I was born knowing something — did that knowledge come from my Guide, from my inner self? It's taken a lifetime to learn to listen to that still small voice above all the cacophony around me. If I'd listened earlier, it could have saved me from my disastrous marriage — so many warnings I chose to ignore! And how can I look at my children and say you are the result of a disaster?

We're all shaped by circumstance to some extent. My Guide suggests there's a meaning to it all and (I hope) a purpose.

At least this last experience has shown me that the answer to it all is love.

N.B. Did I call it a still small voice? It's been shouting at me most of my life!!!

?

What if true life
    and true love,
        lie beyond the jaws of death?

What if we fly out of this darkness into Light?

What if the jaws of death
    are really pelvic bones!?

www.ingramcontent.com/pod-product-compliance
Lightning Source LLC
Chambersburg PA
CBHW042126100526
44587CB00026B/4187